Dressing up as a
KNIGHT

Rebekah Joy Shirley
Photography by Chris Fairclough

This paperback edition printed in 2012 by Franklin Watts

Franklin Watts
338 Euston Road
London NW1 3BH

Franklin Watts Australia
Level 17/207 Kent Street, Sydney, NSW 2000

Produced by Arcturus Publishing Limited,
26/27 Bickels Yard, 151–153 Bermondsey Street, London SE1 3HA

Series concept: Discovery Books Ltd., 2 College Street,
Ludlow, Shropshire, SY8 1AN
www.discoverybooks.net
Managing editor for Discovery Books: Laura Durman
Editor: Rebecca Hunter
Designer: Blink Media
Photography: Chris Fairclough

The author and photographer would like to acknowledge the following for their help in preparing this book: the staff and pupils of Chad Vale Primary School, Cyrus Dhariwal, Rory Munro, Zaydan Law, Abbie Sangha, Oliver Town, Lydia Wright.

A CIP catalogue record for this book is available from the British Library.

Dewey Decimal Classification Number: 646.4'78

ISBN 978 1 4451 1402 6

Printed in China

Franklin Watts is a division of Hachette Children's Books, an Hachette UK company.
www.hachette.co.uk

Supplier 03, Date 0312, Print Run 1798

CONTENTS

Some of the projects in this book may require the use of needles, pins and safety pins. We would advise that young children are supervised by a responsible adult.

KEEP YOUR HEAD!

Knights often fought on the battlefield. They had to protect themselves from **enemies**. Knights needed helmets to protect their heads.

Make a helmet using:

A balloon
A tape measure
Newspaper, torn into strips
Craft glue and a paintbrush
Silver paint and a paintbrush
Silver sequins
Silver fabric
An old cereal packet
A pair of scissors
A ruler

TIP:
If you want to make the glue runnier, mix four teaspoons of water with two tablespoons of glue in a jam jar.

1 Measure around your head with a tape measure. Blow up a balloon so that it is slightly bigger than your head measurement. Cover the top half of the balloon in three layers of newspaper and glue.

2 When the glue is dry, burst the balloon. Tidy the edges of the dome and paint it silver.

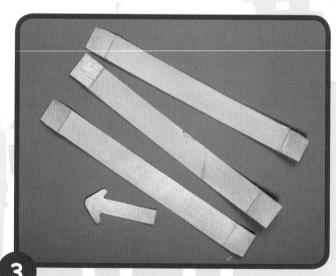

3 Cut three long strips of card (30 cm x 5 cm) from a cereal packet. Cut an arrow-shaped nose guard from the card, too. Paint all the pieces of card silver.

4

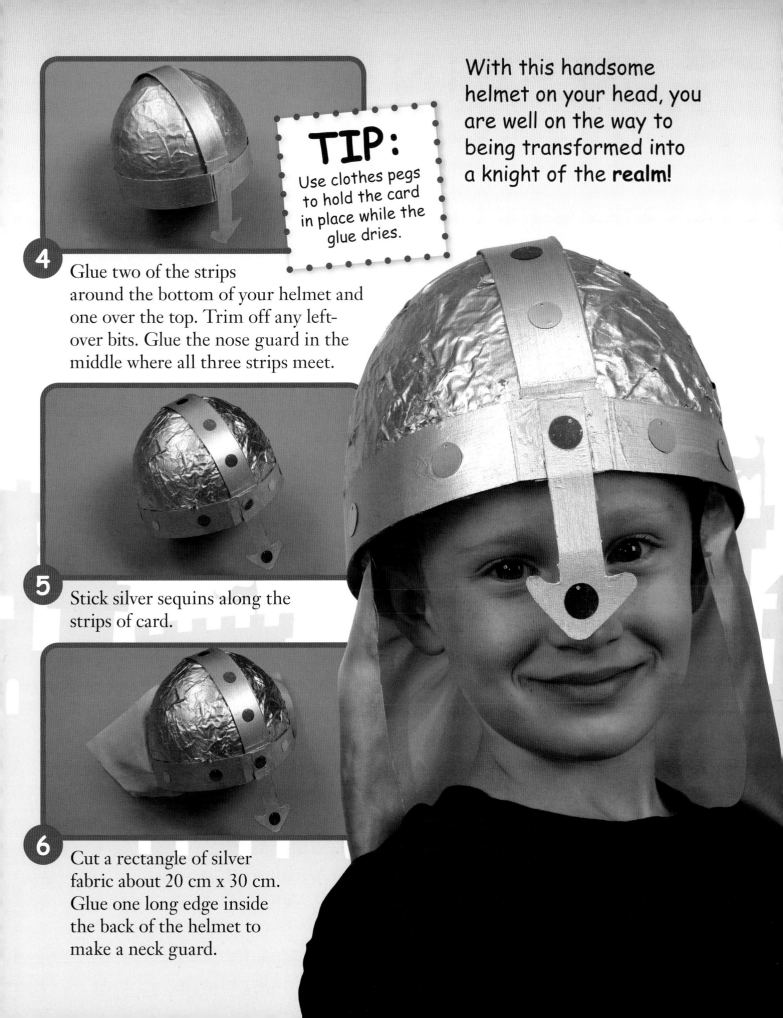

With this handsome helmet on your head, you are well on the way to being transformed into a knight of the **realm!**

TIP:
Use clothes pegs to hold the card in place while the glue dries.

4 Glue two of the strips around the bottom of your helmet and one over the top. Trim off any left-over bits. Glue the nose guard in the middle where all three strips meet.

5 Stick silver sequins along the strips of card.

6 Cut a rectangle of silver fabric about 20 cm x 30 cm. Glue one long edge inside the back of the helmet to make a neck guard.

BEST IN THE VEST!

Knights wore protective vests made of chain mail. Chain mail is made from iron rings linked together in rows.

To make your own chain mail vest you will need:
A grey long-sleeved t-shirt
A black permanent marker pen
A large plastic bottle top

1 Draw around the bottle top in black marker pen to make a curved row of circles on the t-shirt.

2 Draw another row of circles overlapping the first.

TIP:
Put two sheets of newspaper inside your t-shirt to stop the marker pen leaking through to the other side.

6

3 Continuing drawing rows of circles until your t-shirt is covered.

A knight's chain mail **armour** could weigh up to 25 kilograms – that's more than the weight of an average 7-year-old child!

A KNIGHT IN SHINING ARMOUR

A knight's arms, legs, shoulders, elbows and knees were protected by large pieces of metal called plate armour.

Make plate armour using:
Four large plastic bottles
A craft knife
Six paper dust masks
Silver paint and a paintbrush
Elastic
A pair of scissors
A hole punch

1 Ask an adult to cut the tops and bottoms off four plastic bottles to make plastic tubes.

2 Cut the tubes in half lengthways and paint them silver.

3 Paint the dust masks silver.

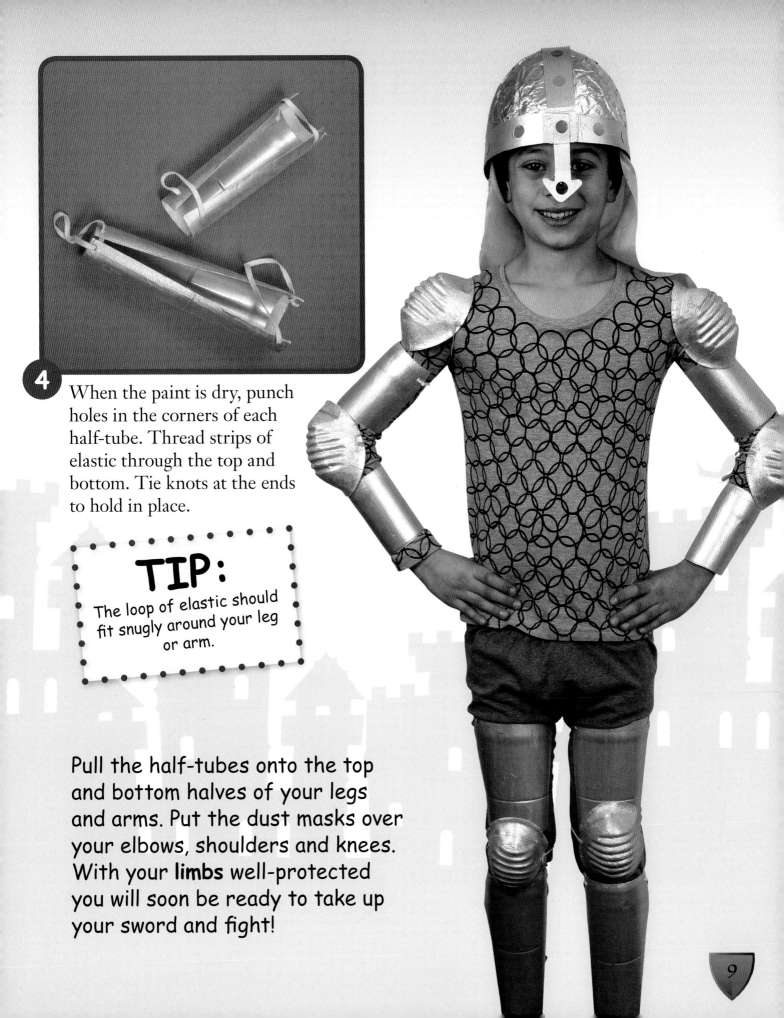

4 When the paint is dry, punch holes in the corners of each half-tube. Thread strips of elastic through the top and bottom. Tie knots at the ends to hold in place.

TIP:
The loop of elastic should fit snugly around your leg or arm.

Pull the half-tubes onto the top and bottom halves of your legs and arms. Put the dust masks over your elbows, shoulders and knees. With your **limbs** well-protected you will soon be ready to take up your sword and fight!

9

A TERRIFIC TABARD

A knight wore another piece of clothing over the top of the chain mail vest called a tabard. The tabard often had a symbol on the front.

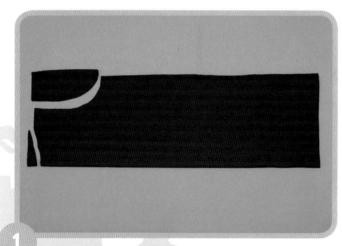

1 Fold a pillowcase in half. Cut the corners off the closed end of the pillowcase as shown in the picture.

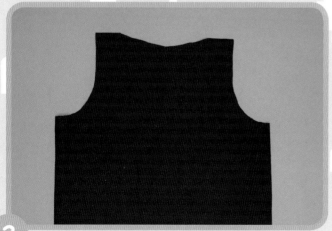

2 Unfold the pillowcase to check the size of the armholes and neck hole you have just made.

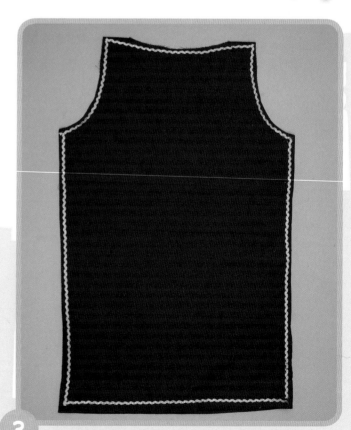

3 Glue gold ribbon around the edges of the pillowcase to make a **border**.

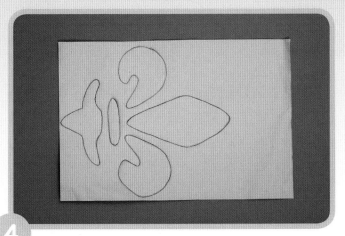

4 Draw a symbol onto the back of the gold paper. The symbol could be a cross, a flower or an animal, such as a lion.

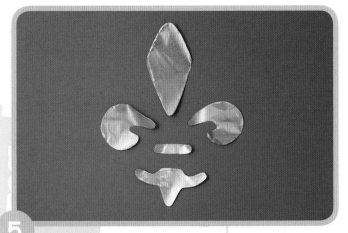

5 Cut the shape out.

6 Glue the shape onto the front of the pillowcase.

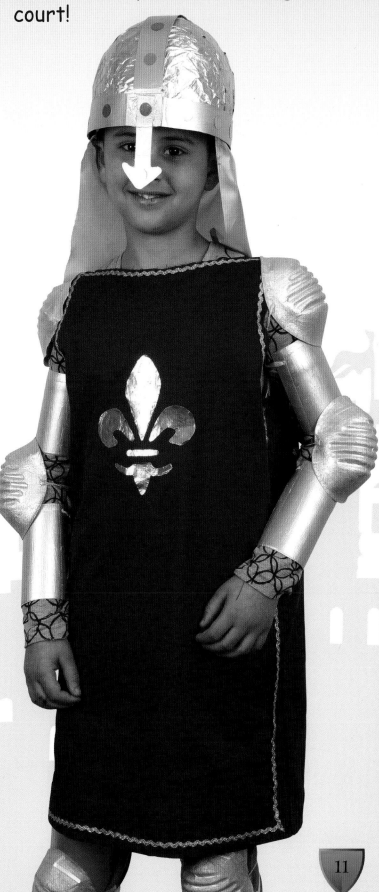

GAUNTLET GLOVES

Knights wore gloves called gauntlets to protect their hands and arms in battle. Gauntlets sometimes had spikes on the wrists to make them look **fearsome**.

To make your gauntlets you will need:
- Thin card
- A pair of scissors
- Black paint and a paintbrush
- A silver pen
- Craft glue and a paintbrush
- A pen or pencil
- A ruler
- A pair of black gloves

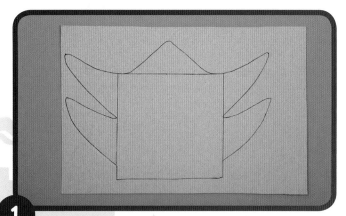

1 Draw a square slightly wider than your wrist onto card (about 10 cm x 10 cm). Draw spikes coming out from the sides of the square and a triangle at one end.

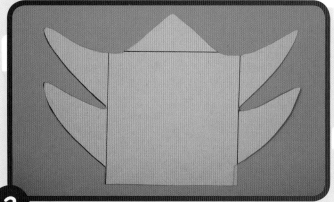

2 Cut the shape out. Use this shape as a template to cut out three more card shapes.

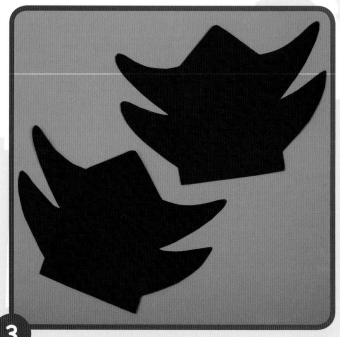

3 Paint all four shapes black.

4 Decorate two of the shapes using a silver pen.

5 Glue the edges of each plain shape to a decorated shape.

When the glue has dried put on your gloves and slip the card shapes over the top. With these smart gauntlets you are ready for a **bout** of **jousting!**

A TRUSTY SWORD

Knights carried sharp, shiny swords which they used to battle with monsters.

To make a sword you will need:
- Cardboard and thin card
- A cardboard tube
- Two plastic bottle tops
- Silver paint and a paintbrush
- Gold paint and a paintbrush
- A pair of scissors
- Sequins
- Craft glue and a paintbrush
- A pen or pencil
- A ruler

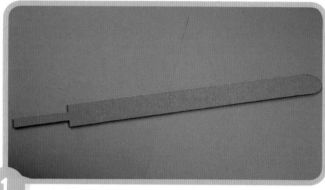

1 Cut a long, thin rectangle of cardboard that is 60 cm long and 6 cm wide. Cut a narrow section at the bottom of the blade to make the handle. It should be the width of the cardboard tube and about 14 cm long.

TIP: Make sure your blade has a rounded end. Otherwise it could be dangerous!

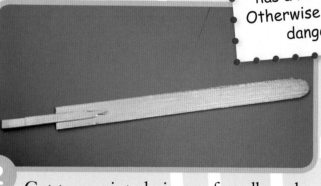

2 Cut two pointed pieces of cardboard the same width as the tube and 28 cm long. Glue them to the handle to strengthen it. Paint the blade silver.

3 Paint the cardboard tube gold and glue a plastic bottle top onto the end.

14

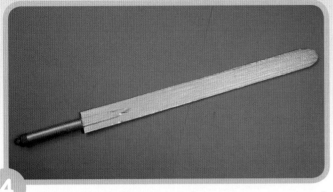

4 Push the tube onto the narrow part of the blade and glue it in place.

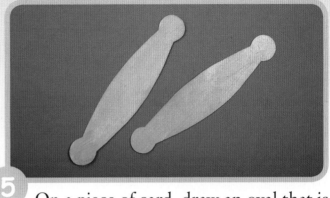

5 On a piece of card, draw an oval that is 18 cm long and 4 cm high. Then draw around a bottle top at each end of the oval. Copy this shape and cut them both out. Paint both shapes gold.

6 Glue the circles at the end of the shapes together to make the **hilt**.

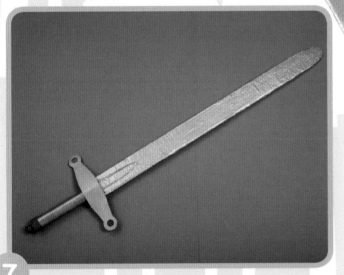

7 Push the hilt over the tube and glue in place where the handle meets the blade. Glue sequins onto each side of the hilt.

Now you are ready to take on a dragon!

A DEFENSIVE SHIELD

Knights used a shield to protect themselves from their enemies' swords.

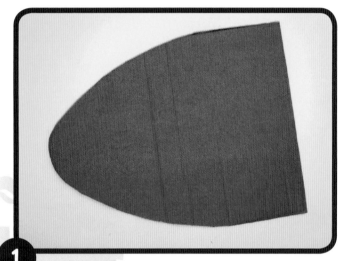

1 Draw a shield shape onto cardboard and cut it out.

2 Paint the shield silver and the string gold. When the paint is dry, glue the string in a pattern around the edge of the shield.

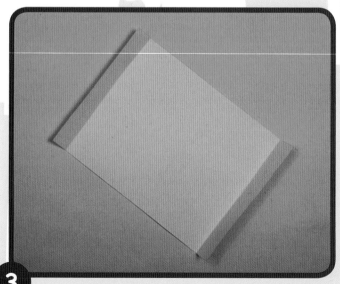

3 Cut a rectangle out of thin card that is around 25 cm long and 17 cm wide. Fold a strip that is 1 cm wide along both of the shorter edges.

4 Glue the folded strips to the back of the shield, making a loop big enough to fit your arm through. This will allow you to hold the shield.

Knights often decorated their shield with a **coat of arms**. Find out how to do this next.

FAMILY PRIDE

A knight's shield bore a design called a coat of arms. This gave information about the history of the family.

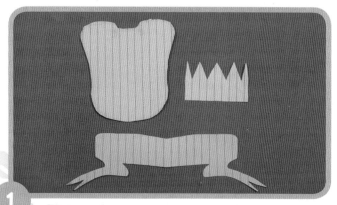

1 Fold a piece of paper in half and draw half a shield shape, a crown and a scroll. Cut them out and unfold the paper. Your shapes will be **symmetrical.**

2 Draw a lion shape on paper and cut it out.

3 Draw around all of the paper shapes on card and cut them out. You will need to draw and cut out two lions.

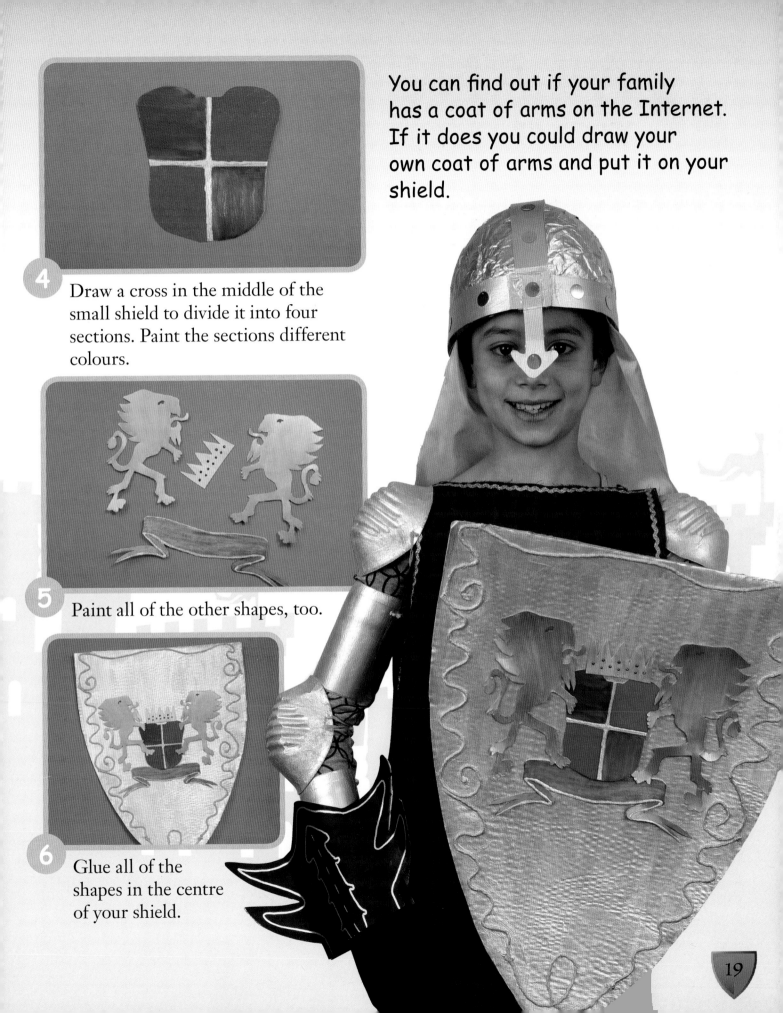

You can find out if your family has a coat of arms on the Internet. If it does you could draw your own coat of arms and put it on your shield.

4 Draw a cross in the middle of the small shield to divide it into four sections. Paint the sections different colours.

5 Paint all of the other shapes, too.

6 Glue all of the shapes in the centre of your shield.

A LANCE FOR LIFE

Knights used to **compete** in jousting games. They charged at each other with a **lance** and tried to knock each other off their horses.

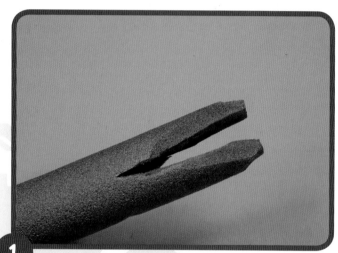

1 Cut a long, thin triangle out of one end of the foam pipe.

TIP:
You could use a small plate to draw around.

2 Stick coloured tape around the pipe at an angle. Use the tape to shape the cut end into a point.

3 Draw a circle onto card and cut it out. The circle should have a diameter of about 15 cm. Cut out a circle the same size as the pipe in the middle.

What do you call a knight that can't stop fighting?
Sir Lance-a-lot!

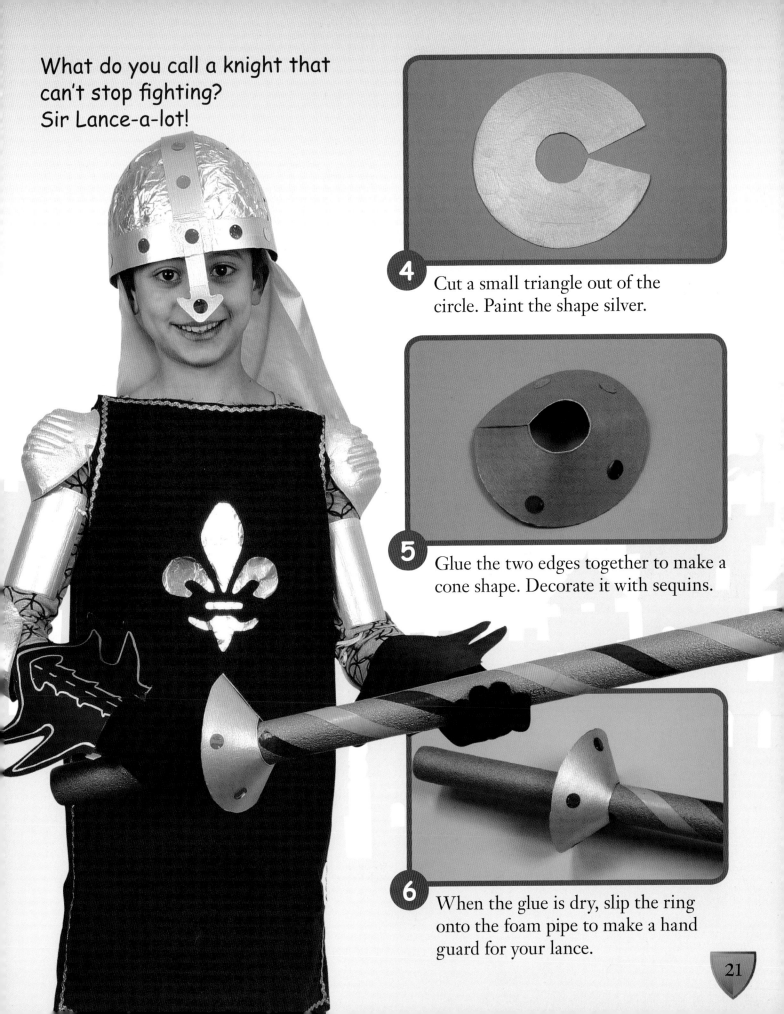

4 Cut a small triangle out of the circle. Paint the shape silver.

5 Glue the two edges together to make a cone shape. Decorate it with sequins.

6 When the glue is dry, slip the ring onto the foam pipe to make a hand guard for your lance.

FLY THE FLAG

Knights often carried flags into battle. The colours of their flag showed which side they were fighting for.

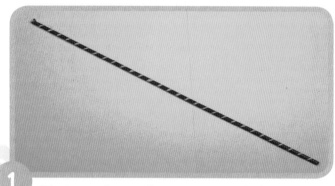

1 Twist coloured tape around the dowel pole.

2 Paint the polystyrene ball gold. Then ask an adult to help you to push it onto the end of the pole.

3 Cut a long triangle out of each length of material. Position the triangles so that one overlaps the other slightly at the widest point and glue them together.

4 Place glue around the edges of the triangles and fold them over.

5 Make a tunnel for the flag pole by folding the side edge over by 2.5 cm and gluing in place.

6 Turn the material over and glue gold ribbon around the edges of the triangles.

7 Guide the dowel pole through the material tunnel.

Wave your flag proudly as you head off to fight for your king and country.

GLOSSARY

armour metal clothing worn for protection
border a strip or pattern around the edge of something
bout a short fight or competition
coat of arms the design on a shield that is linked to a particular family
compete to take part in a competition or game
enemy someone who doesn't like you or wants to harm you
fearsome very frightening
hilt the handle of a sword or dagger
jousting fighting between knights on horseback, using lances
lance a long spear used by knights
limbs arms or legs
realm a country ruled by a king or queen
symmetrical being exactly the same on both sides

FURTHER INFORMATION

Knights and Castles by Rachel Firth (Usborne Activities, 2010)
Knights by Chris Gravett (Dorling Kindersley, 2007)
The Adventures of Sir Gawain the True by Gerald Morris (Houghton Mifflin Harcourt, 2011)
How to Be a Knight by David Steer (Templar Publishing, 2006)

www.earlybritishkingdoms.com/kids/arthur_success.html
Learn about King Arthur and his legendary Knights of the Round Table.
www.knightsandarmor.com/
Enjoy travelling back to the Middle Ages as you explore the world of the medieval knight.
www.yourchildlearns.com/heraldry_activity.htm
This website will show you how to design a traditional medieval shield complete with authentic coat of arms

INDEX